writer
TOM DEFALCO

pencils
PAT OLLIFFE

inks
AL WILLIAMSON

WITH *SAL BUSCEMA* (FINISHES, ANNUAL)

colors
CHRISTIE SCHEELE

letters
DAVE SHARPE

cover art
PAT OLLIFFE

collection editor
JENNIFER GRÜNWALD

senior editor, special projects
JEFF YOUNGQUIST

director of sales
DAVID GABRIEL

production
JERRY KALINOWSKI

book designer
CARRIE BEADLE

creative director
TOM MARVELLI

editor in chief
JOE QUESADA

publisher
DAN BUCKLEY

AVENGING ALLIES

MARVEL COMICS
THE DAUGHTER OF THE TRUE SPIDER-MAN!
SPIDER-GIRL
SEPT #12
APPROVED BY THE COMICS CODE AUTHORITY
DUEL WITH DARKDEVIL!

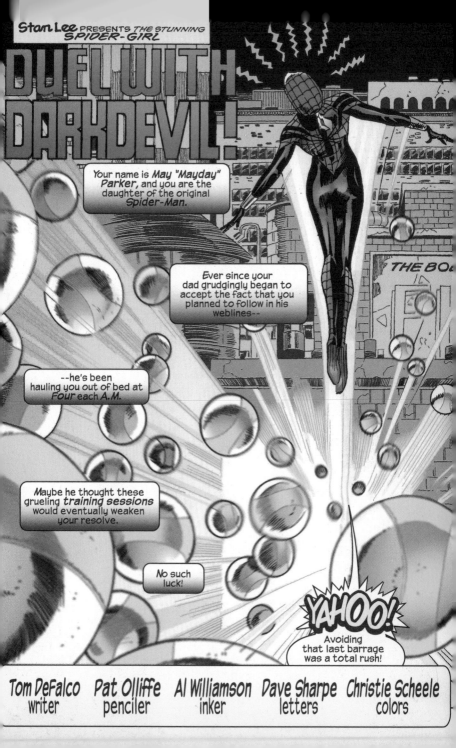

Stan Lee PRESENTS *THE STUNNING SPIDER-GIRL*

DUEL WITH DARKDEVIL!

Your name is *May "Mayday" Parker,* and you are the daughter of the original *Spider-Man.*

Ever since your dad grudgingly began to accept the fact that you planned to follow in his weblines--

--he's been hauling you out of bed at *Four* each A.M.

Maybe he thought these grueling *training sessions* would eventually weaken your resolve.

No such luck!

YAHOO!

Avoiding that last barrage was a total rush!

Tom DeFalco
writer

Pat Olliffe
penciler

Al Williamson
inker

Dave Sharpe
letters

Christie Scheele
colors

Seems like somebody's little girl is finally getting a handle on this web thing.

You okay, dad?

You look a little stressed.

Ahhhh... Problems at work.

You're pretty friendly with *Phil Urich.* He mention anything to you?

He's been acting real strange lately-- taking these long lunches every day.

And he seems-- I don't know--*furtive?* Almost as if he's *hiding* something.

Uh-oh! This is your fault.

While your dad was still in his anti-Spider-Girl phase, Phil volunteered to train you.

The situation may have changed, but you...*you just couldn't ditch your Uncle Phil!*

It never occurred to you that you might be jeopardizing his career.

I... I'm sure it's nothing serious.

Uncle Phil's a good man, dad.

Whatever he's doing... I'm sure he believes it's important.

I hope you're right, hon.

You've got to find a way to repair this rift between your dad and Phil.

MIDTOWN HIGH SCHOOL

But that's a lot easier said than--

Earth to Parker! Have you heard a word I've said?

S-Sorry, Moose. I'm a little distracted today.

What were you asking me?

I was wondering if *Courtney* was seeing anybody these days?

C-Courtney--?!
Y-You're *interested* in Courtney?

Kind'a... *Yeah!*

?!?

Courtney Duran?!

Hey, *Mansfield!*

I don't know what you just said to Mayday, but you obviously upset her.

You'd better apologize to my girl, mister--*and I mean NOW!*

Yo, mister tough guy! You should watch where you're walking!

This was a public corridor the last time I checked.

I'm in a hurry, man!

The rest of the morning passes quickly--

--and you soon find yourself dressing for your regular lunch date with Uncle Phil.

Should you tell him about your father's concerns?

Or just take him off the hot seat, and stop these afternoon training sessions?

Hey! It isn't as if you still need them now that dad's online!

And yet...

NEW & IMPROVED

Uncle Phil is the only one who supported you from the very start.

You can't just dump him!

It wouldn't be fair, right, or-- red alert!

Something's triggered your spider-sense!

Something real nasty by the feel of it!

There! On that distant rooftop-- your old friend Darkdevil!

B-but what's he doing--?

Keep on singing, little birdie! I love the sound of your voice!

I...I've already told you everything I--

ARRRGH!

DAILY BUGLE

That's the rag which used to dog your dad!

Mr. Walters! *Mr. Walters!* I just picked up a hot scoop from one of our stringers. Seems the new *Spider-Girl* just roughed up some poor citizen.

You *sure* about this, Ms. Moore?

More or less! My source saw her with the victim...but he was taken in for treatment before giving a statement.

You keep this story under wraps until you can verify the facts.

Shouldn't we take it to the chief?

Absolutely *not!*

I don't want to risk sparking another *anti-Spider* campaign--

≶Harrumph≷

I still owned this newspaper the last time I checked, Mr. Walters--

--and I'm fully capable of assessing this story on my own.

Gather your facts, Ms. Moore--and I agree with my editor in chief on this point--they must be confirmable *facts* and not mere speculation.

The public has a right to know the *truth* about this new Spider-person.

Is she a SUPER HERO or a SUPER-MENACE?

I'll get right on it, Mr. Jameson!

Shouldn't you be in *school,* young lady?

I'm between classes. My next one doesn't start for a half hour or so.

School was very different in my day.

POLICE
MIDTOWN SOUTH

≈Ahem≈

What can I do for you?

I was...*uhhh*...hanging in the school library, reading up on all the currently active super guys.

Just to, *you know,* check out the competition--and I can't find much about the one they call *Darkdevil.*

Forget him! He's not anyone you want to know.

The guy's a sick and twisted individual.

A flimflam artist who's ripping off the memory of a great man.

And he always speaks so *highly* of you...

Say *wha--?!*

Joke, daddy...
You know anything about an enemy of his named *Cane?*

KAINE--?!

What's this about, May? Where'd you hear that name?

I...I saw it mentioned in... an old newspaper.

That monster has nothing to do with you. Just put him out of your mind!

You should be concentrating on your *schoolwork* instead of wasting time with this nonsense.

I...I gotcha.

Speaking of school, I'd better get moving. We can finish this discussion later.

There's nothing further to discuss, young lady.

Who is Cane?

Why does he inspire such obvious affection?

Does he also have some past history with *Spider-Man*, or is your dad just being his usual overprotective--

May--?!

What are you doing here?

Uncle Phil--!

Your lunch date--!

I'm glad to see you're all right. I got worried when you didn't show at the warehouse.

Something came up, and I had to talk to my father.

Your... father?

Oh, no! Not the hurt puppy dog face!

I...I really have to run.

I'll call you later.

Yeah. Sure.

Everything's set, and all the appropriate palms have been greased.

You're shipping out at midnight on *The Double Clover.*

You won't be late if you know what's good for you.

I assume you know the devil man's been chewing up the entire city, trying to get the bite on you.

Must have been a pretty big score to draw you back here after all these years, and--

¡ARRRK¡

Are you prying into my personal affairs, Weasel?

N-NO, Kaine! N-Not at all!

See that you *don't*...

Because I came to check up on a *family* matter.

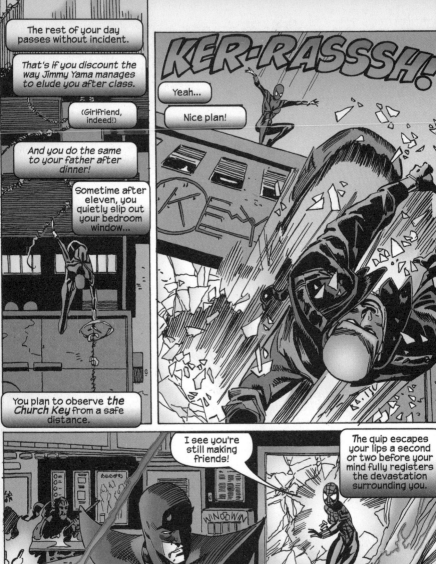

The rest of your day passes without incident.

That's if you discount the way Jimmy Yama manages to elude you after class.

(Girlfriend, indeed!)

And you do the same to your father after dinner!

Sometime after eleven, you quietly slip out your bedroom window...

You plan to observe *the Church Key* from a safe distance.

KER-RASSSH!

Yeah...

Nice plan!

I see you're still making friends!

The quip escapes your lips a second or two before your mind fully registers the devastation surrounding you.

Darkdevil is obviously out of control--

--and must be stopped!

Spider-Girl! I warned you against interfering!

--Whether you like it or NOT!

SKEEE-RASHH!

I don't know where all this newfound confidence has come from, child--

--But it'll only get you HURT!

Seriously HURT!

Maybe not.

I haven't exactly been frittering away my days, watching the soaps!

All right, I'll concede that you've *improved* over the last few months--

--but you're still a beginner compared to *me!*

Playtime is OVER, young lady!

I have a *freighter* to catch, and a *demon* to destroy!

No, Darkdevil! *NO!* I can't let you *go!*

You instinctively raise your hands, failing to notice the chunks of debris that still cling to your palms.

And then--!

I won't let you LEAVE!

PPPHHIP!

How did you manage to discharge that rubble at me?

Neither your father nor I ever--

You--?!

What do *you* have to do with my father?

Never mind! I've already said too much.

Without another word, he takes to the roofs--obviously heading for the wharf!

OLICE
TOWN SOUTH

Catch you tomorrow, Phil.

Have a safe shift, Rizzo.

You planning to go straight home, Uncle Phil?

Or can I con you into a quick pit stop at the diner?

May--?!

What are you doing out so late?

Waiting for you!

I know that this is the night you usually log an extra shift.

You should be *home*, young lady.

Hey! I still have a few hours before I'm due to wake up!

A very few, thanks to your dad!

You simply won't believe the day I had, Uncle Phil.

You know how I can *cling* to walls?

Well, I just learned that's not *all* I can do...

"PH

THE END... for now!

MISERY

Why did *Mr. Slattery* choose today of all days?

(Okay, so maybe he was a little disappointed with your paper on *The Great Gatsby*.)

(Hey, with the early morning practice sessions with your dad, and the late night forays as *Spider-Girl*-- it's a miracle you even finished it!)

Did he really have to see you after class?

Your name is *May "Mayday" Parker*--

--and you're totally smoked at your English teacher for making you so late.

Ron Frenz
story idea

Tom DeFalco
writer

Pat Olliffe
pencil breakdowns

Sal Buscema
finished art

Dave Sharpe
letters

Christie Scheele
colors

Faster, girl! *Faster!*

This could be your only chance to ever catch a glimpse of...of *him!!*

A few months ago you learned that your dad was the amazing *Spider-Man*--

--and that you had somehow *inherited* his spectacular powers.

Remember how excited you were?

That's probably how the rest of this crowd is feeling right now!

MAY! Over here, girlfriend!

Good ol' *Davida*--she and *Courtney* saved you a spot by the barricade!

D-Did I miss any- thing?

Not yet! He's still inside his trailer, and-- *Wait!*

LOOK! The door's starting to open--!

It's *HIM!*

It's really him!

You GO, boy!

Every generation has its movie idols.

Ours just happens to be *Leonard Groote,* the star of *Portrait of a Young Artist* and *The Sensitive Man.*

He's soooooo very gorgeous!

I've had an itch for this boy ever since his days on *Everybody's Happy* with... What *was* her name?

Melissa somebody.

Carsdale, you think--

--even as your *spider-sense* suddenly begins to tingle--

--alerting you to approaching *danger.*

B-but that's ridiculous! Everybody loves Leonard!

(Even your *mom* thinks he's hot!)

Hey! What's with this stupid *smoke?*

It's ruining my *big* entrance!

S-somebody must have screwed up, Mr. Groote!

We didn't schedule any special effects for this shoot!

Hello, Leonard, my darling.

Do you remember me?

There was a time-- *long, long ago*--when we were *co-workers... friends*...and much, much *more!*

You and I shared such beautiful dreams!

We really should have lived happily ever after--

--but then *you* decided to move on--

--without me!

I guess the show's over. We might as well head back to school.

Melissa Carsdale? I used to be jealous of her!

Odd!

Your spider-sense is still tingling.

Why?!

You okay, May? You seem a little distracted. Hope you didn't *buy* that publicity scam!

I'm *sure* it was *real!*

Not a chance!

Miss Parker! *Miss Parker!* May I have a word with you? It's about your paper on *The Great Gatsby!*

But I thought we already came to an agreement, Mr. Slattery!

So did I...until I reread it...and discovered a few paragraphs that were copied *verbatim* from one of your sources! *Unacceptable,* young lady!

Don't you *dare* lie to me! I have *proof*...and you have an F!

B-But I *never*--!

B-but, sir, I--! *Enough!* I already gave your paper to the principal. Take your excuses to *him!*

Gosh, May, I knew your grades have been falling lately, but--*plagiarism?!*

You're in big trouble, girlfriend!

GYMNAS

Stunned and humiliated by this outrageous accusation, you slink away from your friends.

I love everything that mattered to me because of Spider-Man--

--and I'm going to RETURN THE FAVOR!

Not in *this* lifetime, mister!

May, *wait!* You don't have the necessary training or experience to take on a total psycho like the Goblin!

Let her *go*, Peter! She's the hero now!

Listen to Mom!

I beat creepola *once*, and I can do it *again*!

Ever hear of *beginner's luck?!*

THOK

He's *stronger* and much *faster* than you remember!

KRAK

KZAK

KRA

He must've been somewhere in the background while you were fighting *Misery*.

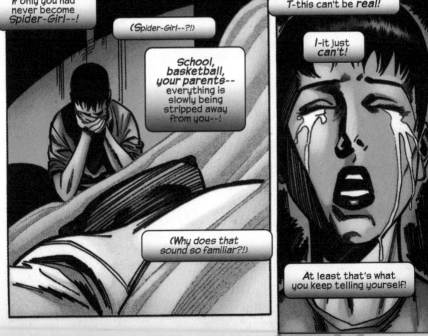

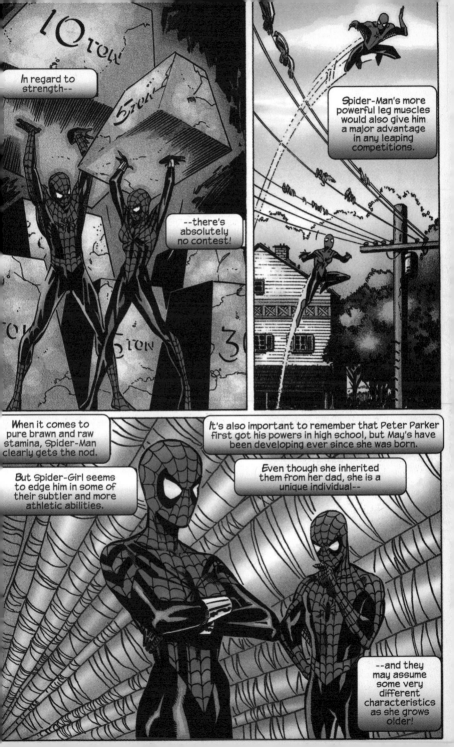

In regard to strength--

--there's absolutely no contest!

Spider-Man's more powerful leg muscles would also give him a major advantage in any leaping competitions.

When it comes to pure brawn and raw stamina, Spider-Man clearly gets the nod.

But Spider-Girl seems to edge him in some of their subtler and more athletic abilities.

It's also important to remember that Peter Parker first got his powers in high school, but May's have been developing ever since she was born.

Even though she inherited them from her dad, she is a unique individual--

--and they may assume some very different characteristics as she grows older!

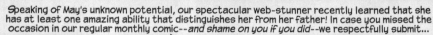

Speaking of May's unknown potential, our spectacular web-stunner recently learned that she has at least one amazing ability that distinguishes her from her father! In case you missed the occasion in our regular monthly comic--*and shame on you if you did*--we respectfully submit...

SPIDER-GIRL'S UNIQUE POWER!

By Tom DeFalco, Pat Olliffe, Josef Rubinstein, Dave Sharpe & Christie Scheele

As you surely know-- unless you spend all your time reading our dreadful competition--both of our Spider-types possess the extra- ordinary ability to cleave to any surface.

Unlike her dad, Spider-Girl needs to focus in order to activate her sticking factor.

(A lapse in concentration can easily result in a severe case of wall-burn!)

To her surprise, May recently discovered that she can use that same act of will to *repel* objects.

If she's already attached to something, she can actually force it to blast away from her.

Okay, maybe this isn't the world's most unusual (or even useful) super-power.

It still gives our nimble neophyte certain bragging rights over daddy dearest--

--and we have a hunch it isn't Mayday's *only* unique power!

T-This can't possibly be **real!**

Duhhh!

You don't have to be a straight-A student to reach that conclusion.

But you should still try you **best.**

I'm counting on you to **win,** Parker--

--and so are **they!**

You can do it, girl!

Make mine Mayday!

You da woman!

MAY

GO, MAY, GO!

35

We're all behind you, May!

What's the hold up, Coach Thompson? Why isn't your player on the court?

Dad--?!

You actually want me to fight my old villains?

Why not?! It's part of a grand **tradition!**

When I was *Spider-Man,* my foes often teamed up against me!

If you really want to follow in my web-steps, you'll get with the program.

Okay OKA

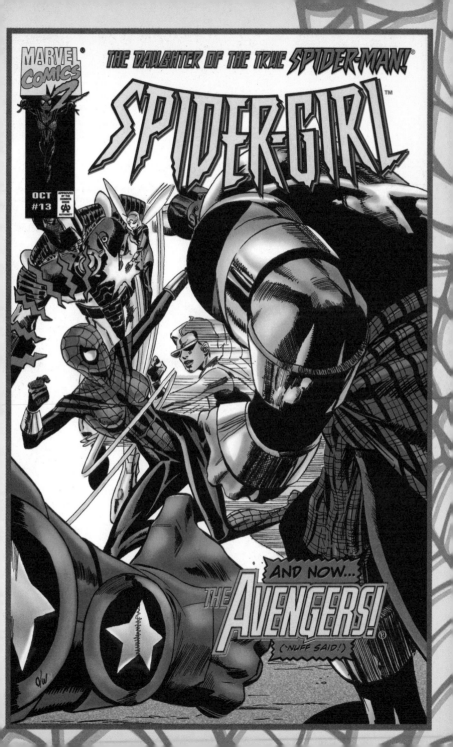

Your dad may have opted for a solitary career, but you've always been a *team* player. Maybe you *should* consider--

Any chance you put in a good word for me?

MIDTOWN HIGH SCHOOL

Oh! Hi, Moose.

I assume you're talking about *Courtney*...

Please don't play with me, Mayday. You gonna help me, or not? I *reallllllly* like her.

Courtney Duran--?!

Why do you sound so surprised?

'Cause you always used to rag on her.

Hey, May--! I thought I heard your voice.

Who are you--oh!

You're in the wrong section, Moose. They keep the comic books with the other periodicals.

I...uhhhhh...I'll catch you later, Mayday. Nice...ummmm...seeing you, Courtney.

SHERMAN

Why are you hanging with that bonehead?

He was telling me about this girl he's into.

Really--?!

Bet she's a vacant-eyed gum-chewer.

Not quite.

She's... *you!*

Me--?!

Moose Mansfield likes *me?*

‡--?!‡

Mayday! Court! I want you guys to meet Ms. Moore.

She's with the Daily Bugle, writing an article on Spider-Girl.

Moose Mansfield--?!

Spider-Girl? Why Spider-Girl?

She's been in the news recently, but there isn't much known about her.

My editor assigned me to gather the facts.

Why bother--? The Bugle's only going to twist them--

--and make her out to be some kind of super-menace!

I can't believe you're helping this woman, Brad.

I thought you liked Spider-Girl.

You mustn't assume I'm doing a negative piece.

Oh, no? Why is Spider-Girl being singled out?

Did you investigate the new Avengers?

I...didn't...but I assume someone must have.

Yeah!

Sure!

I bet!

What's wrong with Brad Miller?

How can he side with the Bugle

--and against you?!

It's a question that continues to gnaw at you--

--until you're *distracted* by your regular afternoon workout with *Phil Urich!*

The clock's *ticking*, May! Let's see how *fast* you run this obstacle course... without the use of your hands.

When you were an active *costumed hero...*

You ever think about joining the Avengers?

I...I guess... but I was never exactly in the *Earth's Mightiest* category.

Not like *you!*

I'm sure they're already scouting you.

Piece of cake! Can I ask you something, Uncle Phil?

Y-You really think so?

I wouldn't be surprised to-- *two minutes, nine point four seconds!* A new record!

Now try it *blindfolded,* and let your *spider-sense* guide you!

WOW! What if Uncle Phil's right? Do you really have the stones to try out for--

Yo, Mayday! How's my girl today?

Your *what*?! Listen, Jimmy... I'm thinking you and I need a *longgggggg* talk.

You've known *Jimmy Yama* most of your life, and he's always been one of your bestest buds--

--but it's time to *off* this "*my girl*" noise!

Uhhhhhh... sure...but I'm a little pushed for time.

I...I'll call you...*okay?*

Guy's no fool.

He can hear the dumpster revving.

Do you *mind*--?!

It's that new kid, again!

What a *creep!*

Sorry, I know this isn't any of my business--

--but I really hope you go *easy* on the poor sap!

There are *worse* things in life...than being *admired.*

A creep...

But a *sensitive* creep!

HA HA HA HA HA HA!

Was it something I said, *Mister* Richards?

I ÷giggle÷ I'm *sorry!* It's just that those Avengers guys act more like a *frat house* than a *super team.*

I ever tell you how they messed up a simple milk run to *Latveria?*

Why would you even consider *them?*

You know any *other teams* I could join?

-- saaaaaay... Isn't that *Nova* streaking toward the Bronx?

Okay, so **why** are you here? **What** do you want?

I was kind'a wondering if you had any...

...openings?

This is how you apply for membership--?

What am I supposed to do--e-**mail** a résumé?! Get letters of recommendation from all the baddies I've clobbered?!

C'mon, Stinger...I say the little lady deserves **props** for initiative! She certainly assembled **us** in a hurry.

Down, Freebooter... Or I'll start reciting synonyms for "**jailbait**"!

As much as I admire everything I've heard about Spider-Girl, we've already experienced way too many **changes** in the past few weeks.*

*As shown in A-Next #11 & #12!

J2 has a point-- --But her unique powers would certainly increase our **offensive capabilities!**

She would have to consent to a complete background check.

Uhhh, guys... I think we should continue this discussion in private!

Even as the Avengers move off, you struggle to maintain your composure.

(Collapsing in a nervous heap won't sell your case!)

Do you really want *this*, little girl?

You can't be a *part-time* Avenger.

You must be willing to drop *everything* whenever summoned.

Family, school and friends-- EVERYTHING!

Are you truly willing to make such a *commitment*?!

≈Ahem≈ I...I'm afraid I have bad news.

The bottom line--we're just not ready to add a new member!

I...*understand!* Thanks for considering me.

≈WHEW≈

We'll try to contact you when we change our minds...

...*if* you're willing to submit to a little *test!*

Test?! What kind of test?

Interesting! You've used a nice variety of tricks and powers against each member.

Boring, I'm not!

How do you plan to secure my flag?

I... I'm not sure... yet!

I'd love to con you into thinking I'm a *master strategist.*

Truth is-- I'm pure *ad lib!*

I just follow my instincts, and react to each new situation as it comes!

And right now they say you need a face full of webbing!

You realize, of course, that an increase in my external temperature will free me within *seconds.*

SSS SSS

You...*lost!*

Lost!

Why so *down,* Spider-Girl? You did *fabulously!*

Even though you *snookered* me, I think you're real *cooooool!*

Y-You *mean--?!*

While we're still not ready to expand our membership, we all agree--

--that we'd be real proud for you to become our first official *Reserve Avenger!*

YAHOOOO!

Pending a full security clearance, of course.

A Reserve Avenger!

Not bad, little girl!

At least one part of your life is finally coming together!

Hey, Jimmy! Wha'cha doing out here?

I...I've just been hanging around...hoping to catch you...and clear the air.

I guess I've been acting like a real *jerk* lately.

Yeah...

...*major league!*

I...

I'm sorry, May.

I never meant to creep you out.

A girl like you deserves *better* than an ugly geek like me.

Jimmy Yama, you are *sooooooo* full of big brown *bull chips--!*

MARVEL COMICS
THE DAUGHTER OF THE TRUE SPIDER-MAN!
SPIDER-GIRL
#14
DEFEATED AND DISGRACED...
...BY THE MAN NAMED KAINE!

Stan Lee presents the ever-stunning SPIDER-GIRL!
The cold rain suddenly jolts you awake--!
(That's when you first realize you've been dozing.)
Time to head home, little girl!
Falling asleep in the middle of a web-swing could be real hazardous to your health.
You can continue your hunt for the currently elusive Darkdevil tomorrow night--
--when you're better rested and the weather's more cooperative.
A MAN CALLED... KAINE!
Your name is May "Mayday" Parker, and you're the daughter of the original Spider-Man.
Even as you veer toward Forest Hills--and the comfort of a warm bed--the old Parker luck suddenly kicks in as gunfire roars in the night.
Tom DeFalco writer
Pat Olliffe penciler
Al Williamson inker
Dave Sharpe letters
Christie Scheele colors

You search for another twenty minutes before finally calling it a night.

Where is *Darkdevil*, anyway?

He used to pop up frequently, trying to discourage you from doing the hero thing.

But you haven't seen him in weeks.

Not since the two of you fought over some stupid super-villain.*

Some guy called...*Cane?*

Or is it *Caine?*

Whatever! It's too late to worry about that now!

You check the hallway before hitting the sheets--

--trying to sense if your parents are still awake--

--praying that your spider-sense won't tingle!

Uh-oh! Only an hour and a half until your father drags you out of bed for your morning training session.

Might as well make the most of it...

But your mind refuses to shut down.

What's happened to Darkdevil?

Is he just ducking you, or...

Rise'n'shine, hotshot!

Time to give the neighbors a break from your snoring.

I... I don't snore... do I?

Even worse than your father!

C'mon--get moving!

It's almost seven-thirty, and you have to get ready for school.

‡kltpzyxm‡

W-Where's Dad?

Why didn't he wake me for our usual *spider-lesson?*

He had a breakfast meeting at the *police lab*--

--and figured you could both use the extra sleep.

Odd! Your father rarely reports to work so early.

He must be on a big case.

Maybe it's related to...*Nah!*

Darkdevil couldn't be involved.

Could he?

MIDTOWN HIGH SCHOOL

YO, Mayday!

Hi, Jimmy.

I....uhhh...want to thank you for taking the time to straighten me out the other day.

Couldn't have been easy for you.

No sweat, Jimmy!

What's the point of having friends if you can't depend on them to tell you when you're acting like a jerk?

There's *Mansfield!* I owe him an apology, too.

Maybe you should just avoid him.

No, I want to get this over with.

Got a minute, Moose?

Don't start with me, Yama! I've had enough grief from you.

I...I know...and I...I'm real *sorry* for the way I've been yanking you.

I've been a major fool, and I hope you can forgive me someday.

Forgive you?

HA!

I'll do better than that, Yama my man!

You and I are about to become *best buds!*

Ask your father!

I have no wish to harm you, child.

This is you trying to *avoid* hurting me--?

≶HOO-boy≶

I want you to deliver a message to your father. Tell him that I, like *Rumplestilskin*, have finally returned to claim my prize.

Isn't he the one *who*--?!

Exactly!

One *other* thing...

Uh-oh! Too late!

'Morning, hotshot! I know it's only *Saturday*, but your father's downstairs, stirring up a batch of his special pancake batter.

Though your parents are aware of the fact that you inherited your dad's amazing spider-like powers--

--they don't know that you've been secretly slipping out at night to do your web thing.

Will you be joining us for--

Oh, God!

At least, they *didn't* know.

You expect an angry stream of *I-told-you-sos*.

A self-righteous condemnation for going behind their backs!

Instead, you get a terrible silence--

--and a face full of fear.

Listen, Mom.

It's really not as *bad* as it looks.

I...I'll tell your father that you're sleeping in.

Y-You'd better stay up here until I can get him out of the house.

Yeah.

Okay.

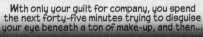

With only your guilt for company, you spend the next forty-five minutes trying to disguise your eye beneath a ton of make-up, and then...

Where'd Dad go?

The station house.

The whole department's been called in to work on a big case.

Mom...we have to talk.

No. Not now.

I'm not ready.

But I'm okay... *really!*

This time!

I know what's coming, May.

I've already lived through it with your father.

I...I've tried to prepare myself.

B-But I'm just not ready.

Screaming would be easier to handle!

Much, much *easier!*

Your father retired from the web biz after he lost his leg.

He now works in the *police lab.*

Your gut tells you that his big case has to do with a certain super-powered *derangeoid* called *Kaine.*

The very same Kaine who completely *overwhelmed* you last night!

You are so lucky to be alive! The guy could have killed you, and--

HELP PPP!

H-He's got my PURSE!

Shut up, you old bag!

For a moment, you stand *frozen--!*

Should you change into *Spider-Girl?*

Is this the only type of crime you're capable of stopping?

We're going *shoe shopping!* Fingeroth's is having a sale-- 40% off!

Forty percent--?!

See? You're already perking up!

Those stilettos are so five minutes ago----but the slides are to die for!

I'm thinking that brown pair would go great with my new--*o-boy!*

Check out the love connection!

Am I the only one who keeps getting weirded out by the sight of *Moose Mansfield* hitting on *Courtney Duran?*

The weird factor is about to hit the red zone. Look *who's* joining them!

Didn't I see you kids at *Midtown High* the other day?

My name is *Moore,* and I work for the *Daily Bugle.*

Yeah, you're the reporter who's trying to dig up the dirt on *Spider-Girl.*

Boy! That sister sure picked the **wrong** two!

Why do you say that, Davida?

You haven't heard why **jock-for-brains** is suddenly so hot for **Nerd Girl?**

Sale 50%

Moose thinks Courtney is **Spider-Girl!**

So... He **is** using her.

Kind'a. Sort'a.

Brad Miller gave me the scoop. He didn't clue you--?

Maybe he's still steaming over your new guy!

New g--you mean JJ?! You're just **busting!**

You **heard** me, lady. **Take a hike!**

Spider-Girl's a real **hero!** She saved my **life** on more than one occasion--and plenty of **others** can say the **same!**

I ain't gonna help the **Bugle** do a hatchet job!

Why do you assume I'll write a **negative piece?**

I'm merely going to report the **facts.**

Like she really has a chance for a fair shake!

Hey, guys-- LOOK! **LOOK!**

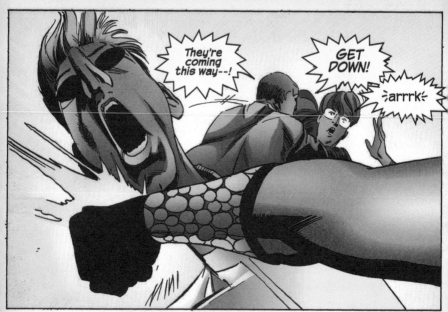

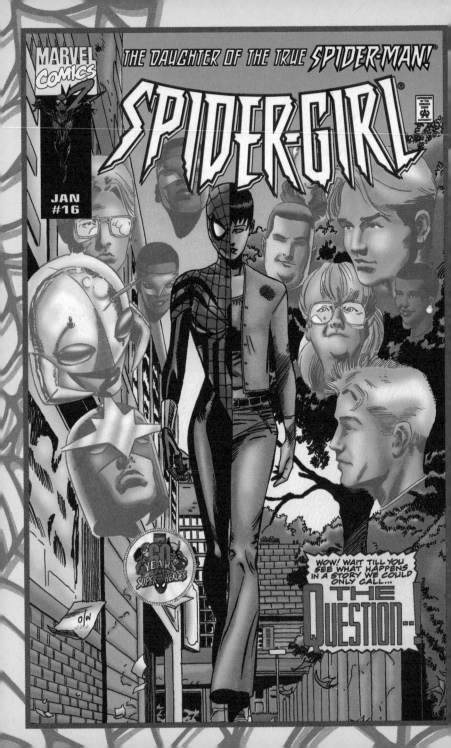

I...I'm fine... if a little embarrassed. Gotta admit that was a good shot.

Mind if I ask why you guys are targeting *Kaine?*

The man's *crazy*-- --the way he's been bloodying up the streets--

--with his one-man *gang war* against the Kingpin of crime!

We don't object to him taking out rival gangsters, but it's only a matter of time before innocent bystanders are caught in the crossfire.

Dirtbags like him are *why* my sister and I--

Whoa! Whoa! Let's not share too much.

Mind if I get up close and personal?

Like, why even bother to play hero if you're not goin' after the Kaines of this world?

Wellllll, I have these real nifty super-powers...

And, like the man says, with great power-- --there should also come-- --great, *uhhh,* responsibility.

Should...but rarely *does!* Just ask *Doctor Doom,* the *Kingpin* or *Kaine.*

You need to lay off the fortune cookies, girl-- --and get yourself a real *mission statement!*

What a pair of *wastes!*

We'll get rich selling dupes of this tape to every guy in school!

And think of the possibilities for blackmail!

While they're certainly not in the *Kaine* category--

--they need to be *stopped.*

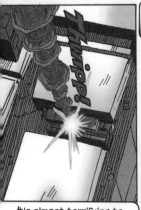

Thwipp!

It's almost terrifying to think guys like that will eventually be contributing to the gene pool.

Or at least *humiliated!*

You wonder how the other boys will react when they find this in *their* locker room.

Hardly the greatest challenge you've ever faced--

--but a Spider-Girl's gotta do what a Spider-Girl's gotta do!

"Hey, Mayday! I couldn't help overhearing the Coach scorch you."

"Don't let him get you down!"

"Basketball lost its thrill the moment you slung your first web, and--Hhhhhhey!"

"He gives everyone the same *best effort* speech at some point or another."

"Brad's just trying to be supportive..."

"Too bad Thompson's right!"

"Since when does JJhang with *Turtle* and *Ralphie?*"

"Not sure...but this isn't the first time I've seen them together."

"What do you expect? Told you he was trouble!"

"Remind me to listen to you more often!"

"Oh, yeah--? Yeah! The guy has a bad rep."

"Thinks he's so cool 'cause his--"

"HEY! HEY! You CRAZY, man?!"

Shame, ladies! Shame on you!

A super hero is supposed to be a role model, with a sacred responsibility to act in a mature and virtuous manner at all times.

Look at the mess you've made! The property you've damaged!

What if *children* saw you, and *imitated* your reckless behavior?!

I expect you to *apologize* to the owner of this garden, and to make full *restitution* for the wreckage you've caused!

You'd better clean up your act, ladies.

I'm going to keep an eye on you!

What a *marooooon!*

Could he *be* a bigger stiff?!

Twenty minutes later, after straightening up the garden, and compensating the owner (who assesses the damage at two chipped flowerpots and a bent trowel) you bid *Stinger* a fond farewell--

--and return to what you laughingly refer to as your *"real"* life.

Earth to Parker--!

Wait up, Mayday! *Wait up--!*

We got hot news, girl.

Moose and Brad dug up some juicy dirt.

SPECIALS
QUICHE
SEAFOOD BISQUE
PAN ROASTED COD
GRILLED CHICKEN
VEGETARIAN PLATE

This about JJ's fight--?

You won't believe it.

We cornered Ralphie Hicks after school.

Yeah, and the little weasel sang like a canary!

JJ threw down on Ralphie and Turtle-- --'cause they said they planted a video cam in the girls locker room.

Only--*get this*--dumb and dumber bugged the *wrong* room!

The entire football team is now gunning for 'em!

JJ...is... *innocent?!*